Contents

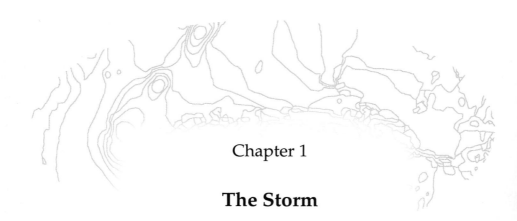

Chapter 1

The Storm

Staring out the window of the space habitat was the perfect way to start the day. Even after all my time on Mars, I still hadn't gotten used to the view: the swirls of red dust with the seventeen-mile-high mountain Olympus Mons in the distance. This view was even more comforting with the hum of the habitat's power system in the background.

My team and I had been stationed here for four months. The government had been planning for decades to send humans to live on Mars. After years of work, researchers had developed the capability to send a group of scientists to the planet. We were that group, and I was the commander. It is our job to make sure the land on Mars is safe for human living.

Over the course of our time on Mars, we've been studying the ground, minerals, atmosphere, and living conditions of the planet. From all we've seen, the Red Planet is a safe place to live. Then again, we've been wearing professionally made safety gear, and we've also had the protection of our space habitat.

ONE MORNING ON MARS

Katie Mastromattei

Art by Jeff Crowther

Literacy Consultants
David Booth • Kathleen Corrigan

However, some of our studies have not been so encouraging. We'd been studying how a vehicle might be engineered to travel long distances on Mars. We needed an all-terrain vehicle to get around the deep craters of the surface, and we needed an aircraft to soar over the planet's mountains. But we were having no luck; it seemed impossible to travel more than a few miles from our habitat before the battery started to die or the harsh terrain of Mars forced us to head back.

It isn't just the surface of Mars that is threatening either. The atmosphere is very thin, the air is very cold, and the water is toxic to humans. In our space habitat we are able to drink water because we have a system that recycles fresh water brought from Earth. Having fresh water means that we can even make coffee. One of my favorite things to do in the morning is to have a cup while looking out the window.

"Commander, how's the planet looking this morning?" I turned my head and saw Arnold, our chemist and second commander. He was pouring himself a mug of coffee.

"Red." I smiled.

"It's been windy so far," Arnold said. "I don't know that we'll be able to go out anytime soon. Did you hear the dust hitting the window this morning? It even woke me up!"

The winds on Mars can be pretty strong. To stay safe, our rule has been to wait an hour after a storm before heading outside of the space habitat.

"At least it will give us more time to finish up those tests that we started on the plants," Arnold said.

We had been experimenting with growing different crops in the greenhouse that we'd set up. After harvesting the crops, we then tested them to see if they contained any minerals that might be harmful to humans. So far we have grown radishes, peas, and tomatoes. We haven't detected any harmful minerals in the vegetables. What's more, they taste almost as good as they do on Earth, even though they've been grown more than fifty million miles away.

Just as we were standing up to walk to the greenhouse, the lights in the station started to flicker. A loud noise made me jump, and then half of the lights shut off. The hum in the station got much quieter.

My team and I have been trained for almost any emergency. Luckily we haven't encountered any in the last four months. This was probably just an electrical problem, but it would take our entire crew to figure out how to fix it.

Moments after the lights went out, the other two members of our crew emerged from their bunks. Arnold and I said good morning to Jessica, our biologist, and Martin, our engineer.

"Why did the lights go out? Commander, is this going to be an easy fix?" Jessica asked.

"I'm not sure why they went out, but we'll figure it out. The wind has been really blowing this morning; maybe something got damaged outside." I felt sure that we would be able to find the problem and fix it, but Jessica didn't look quite so convinced.

"OK, let's go see what we can find," she said.

Jessica met Martin and Arnold at the circuit breaker panel. Meanwhile, I tried to start communication with mission control; our team on the ground might have been able to see damage to the habitat from one of their satellites even if we couldn't see it from inside.

I dialed in the frequency for mission control, but our video screen remained blank. I knew we were in trouble because the blank screen meant that we'd lost our satellite connection with Earth. Martin began working at the video screen's control panel just in case this was only a problem with the screen's display.

We needed to establish a connection with Earth; if we couldn't, we wouldn't be able to get satellite images of the damage to our habitat. The problem could then quickly become an emergency.

Suddenly the speakers connected to the screen came to life.

"Hello there. Can you hear us?" A voice that I couldn't recognize crackled through the speakers.

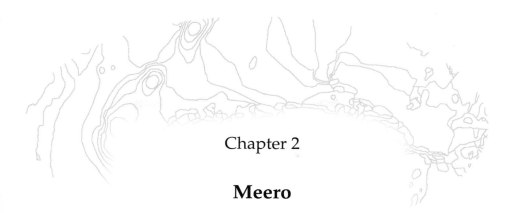

Chapter 2

Meero

"This is Meero," said the voice from the speaker. "I live five miles away, and we received the distress signal from your station. It appears that the dust storm damaged your power center."

I was shocked! This was actual contact from life on Mars! We knew that life-forms existed on the planet, as the Mars rover had taken photos of their dwellings. We had been trying to establish contact with them during our time here, but we'd had no luck. Now they were reaching out to us.

"Um, hello, Meero. This is the commander of the mission." My voice was shaking. I couldn't believe I was actually talking to a Martian! "Half of our lights have gone out, and the station seems to be losing its satellite signal and electricity. Can you tell how much damage has been done to our power center?"

The Mars rover photos showed us that the Mars dwellers have excellent technological capabilities. I was hoping that Meero would be able to help us fix our station. Once that was solved, perhaps he could show us how they engineered vehicles to get around on Mars.

"Commander, our signals are showing that your power center has sustained a great deal of damage," Meero replied. "You will lose power in two hours. You will need to get into your safety suits and prepare to leave your base and come with us."

This was bad news. Humans are not able to survive on Mars outside of a habitat like ours because the atmosphere is too thin. The space suits we'd been given could provide us with only enough oxygen to last for one day. Our entire crew knew that leaving the habitat was very dangerous.

"Is your living space safe for humans?" asked Jessica with some concern.

"The air in our living quarters is the same as the atmosphere on Mars, so you would not normally survive in it. However, we do have a vaccine that can assist you with that. It was developed to help humans adapt to the environment here on our planet."

This was shocking news. How did they know so much about humans? We had been on the planet for only four months — how had they developed the vaccine in such a short time?

"If you invite us into your base, we can give you the vaccine," Meero continued. "Then we can teach you how to survive until your team on Earth can send help."

My crew looked at one another nervously. We knew that taking the vaccine would be the only way for us to survive here. The journey to Mars takes over a year, and we would not live long enough for a rescue mission to come for us.

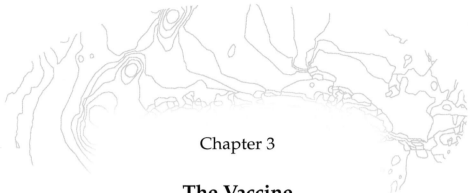

Chapter 3

The Vaccine

We nervously watched the feed from the camera outside the habitat — the only device that luckily still had power. Eventually, two figures emerged from the swirling dust. They moved easily over the ground, taking giant steps, and they soon reached the air lock of the habitat. I nodded to Arnold, and he pressed the button that opened the air lock.

When the two Martians entered the habitat, Meero introduced himself first. He looked similar to us, to my surprise, but with longer extremities. His skin was gray, and when he blinked, I could see that he had two layers of eyelids.

Meero introduced the figure standing beside him; it was his sister, Issta. We greeted them both warmly.

Meero showed us the vaccine that we would need to take. It was a bright orange liquid that swirled around inside a clear, grape-sized capsule.

"The first thing you will notice is that your breathing will change. This will help you to survive in the low level of oxygen in our atmosphere," Issta explained. "You will move slowly at first. In a few days, though, you should be able to run and jump just as you could on Earth."

"Next, the vaccine will keep the core temperature of your body at a normal level. It will do this without reducing your blood flow or making you shiver, as

would happen on Earth," Meero explained. "This is so that you can survive in the extreme cold of our planet. The temperature here sometimes goes down to eighty degrees below freezing." Just hearing the temperature made Jessica shiver and rub her hands together.

"How long will it take for the vaccine to work? When will we be able to leave the habitat safely?" I asked.

"In one hour you will be ready to leave in your space suits, and you can come with us to our living quarters. The oxygen in your suits should last you until tomorrow. After that, we can go outside and teach you some skills that will make living on Mars much easier."

As commander, I felt it was my duty and my responsibility to be the first to take the capsule. I extended my hand, and Issta handed me the capsule. I hesitated for a second or two, but then chewed the capsule slowly. I cringed and then smiled. "It's a bit sour, but it kind of tastes like candy," I concluded. We all laughed.

Issta handed out the rest of the capsules. As each of the members of my crew chewed the capsules, I wondered if the four of us would end up looking like Meero and Issta once the vaccine did its job.

I didn't get to dwell on that thought for very long before a loud screeching noise made us jump. Then a thump sounded, and the lights dimmed even more.

"The power is shutting down," said Martin, concerned. "I'd say we have another hour before it cuts out completely."

"You should take one last look around the station and pack up anything that you'll need for a few days," Meero said. "We'll all come back for the rest once you've fully adapted to the environment." He sounded certain the vaccine would work, but this wasn't enough to put me at ease.

Carefully, the four of us, with the help of Meero and Issta, put dehydrated food, medication, and tools in our packs. We were moving slower than usual, the vaccine already doing its work. As I looked around the habitat, I wondered if we would all be the same when we returned.

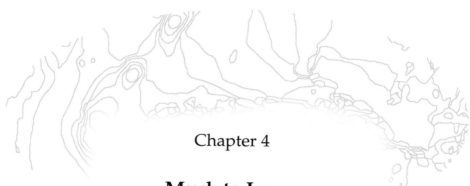

Chapter 4

Much to Learn

An hour later, Issta led the way out of the habitat. We all made our way along the dusty ground toward the mysterious living quarters of our new friends. I noticed that Meero and Issta bounced higher than we did when they walked. It looked as though they were walking on a trampoline. I also noticed for the first time that they had small webs under their arms.

It was a long walk, but Meero was right; our breathing was starting to feel different. It wasn't hard to carry all of our supplies, and we were walking faster. No one was complaining about the cold either. Normally we would feel a little chill when we left the habitat. Now, though, we were all feeling comfortably warm. I was trusting the vaccine more by the minute, which brought me great relief.

When we arrived at Meero and Issta's living space, we were amazed to find that it was similar to the one we had just left. It was the same size and color as ours, and it had similar types of furniture and technology. Meero showed us that the windows in their home opened and closed so that if the wind was calm, they could get some fresh air. He explained that their skin was thicker than ours, which meant that the cold had no effect on them. Soon my crew and I would be able to sit and enjoy the fresh air, too, without the weight of our space suits.

We'd been up for only a few hours, but the long walk had exhausted us. Meero explained that this was perfectly natural, as fatigue was one of the first side effects of the vaccine. He took each of us to a bunk where we could get some sleep while the vaccine completed its work on our bodies. He told us we should remove our space suits in the morning.

Before I entered my bunk, I turned to Meero and asked him why anyone on Mars would have developed a vaccine for human beings.

"Issta and I are scientists much as you are," he said. "We watched your rover explore our planet for years, and we knew that human beings would not be far behind. We developed the vaccine so that, when you did come, you could live side by side with us."

I couldn't contain my enthusiasm. "You're both scientists? My crew and I have so much to learn from you!"

"And we have so much to learn from you," Meero said with a smile.

I told Meero that I had many questions for him, but that I would leave them for later.

"Until tomorrow," we said to each other, and I turned off the light.

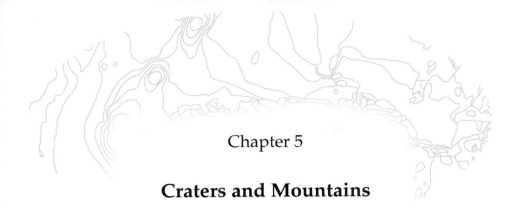

Chapter 5

Craters and Mountains

When I woke up, I removed my space suit with caution and immediately felt that my breathing was regular. Stepping out of bed, I noticed that my legs felt stronger as well. That was a surprise as we hadn't been told anything about this effect of the vaccine. I made my way to the common area, where Meero and Issta were waiting for all of us.

"You must be well rested after twenty hours of sleep," Issta said. None of us could believe we'd been out that long, but she explained that it was perfectly natural.

During breakfast I took the opportunity to thank our friends for their hospitality, and then got on to my big question.

"I wish we had made contact before, but our vehicle never would have made it this far," I began.

"We simply can't figure out how to build ground or air vehicles that will carry us long distances." I looked at my fellow crew members. "We were wondering, well, would you be willing to share your engineering secrets with us?"

Meero and Issta exchanged smiles with each other. "Come with us," Meero said.

We followed them out of the building and immediately felt the air on our skin.

"Do you feel cold at all?" asked Meero.

"Not at all. I'm very comfortable," Martin said. The air felt as natural to us in our everyday clothes as it had when we were in our space suits the day before.

"These are good signs," Issta said. "The vaccine was definitely a success." Issta could not hide her excitement.

When we were all gathered together, Meero announced that he had something to demonstrate for us. He then crouched down before leaping up and soaring almost a mile into the air.

"Amazing!" Jessica exclaimed.

"How did you do that?" I asked.

"Meero and I were born with springs in our heels. Jumping like this is easy for us," Issta explained.

"But now we'd like you to try something," said Meero. "Bend your knees and jump!"

All four of us did what he said. When we jumped, we leapt up almost half as high as Meero and Issta had.

"This is incredible!" Arnold whooped.

"How are we doing this?" asked Martin.

Issta tried to get us to stand still so that she could explain everything to us, but we were too excited to stop jumping. Eventually she gave up and started talking to us as we jumped up and down.

"The vaccine we gave you has strengthened the muscles in your legs," Issta said. "We who live on Mars have springs in our heels so that we can easily make it over the craters and valleys on our planet. Some of them are six miles deep, and we would never be able to climb out of them without springs."

"What if you get stuck in the craters?" asked Martin.

Meero smiled. He lifted his arms above his head, and the translucent webbing under his arms became a shiny film that spread from his sides to his wrists. He bent his knees slowly, and then he bounced twice. He quickly started to move his arms up and down, and eventually his body lifted right off the ground. Once he was in the air, he stopped flapping his arms and soared through the sky, the wind blowing through his wings. I couldn't believe what I was seeing. I looked at Arnold and saw that his mouth had dropped open, as had Martin's and Jessica's.

"Please tell me we can do that too!" Arnold exclaimed. Everyone laughed.

Meero and Issta explained that the vaccine they'd given us couldn't let us fly. The people of Mars had developed these wings over thousands of years as an adaptation to the landscape of their planet. Besides deep craters, Mars is covered in mountains and volcanoes, and the wings allow the people of the planet to fly over them.

So this was why we hadn't been able to figure out the mystery of getting around on Mars. People hadn't used technology to master their environment; their bodies had developed in ways that did this for them.

"Our bodies have developed in other ways too," Issta said from high up in the air. "For instance, it's very easy for us to carry other life-forms." She smiled. "What do you say? Would you like to see more of Mars than you ever could have from a scientific base?"

"Really? You could do that for us?" I asked excitedly.

With that, Issta swooped down and lifted me up by my underarms. I let out a laugh as she whisked me high into the air. At the same time, Meero picked Arnold up. They told Martin and Jessica that they'd be back for them soon, and our crewmates waved to us from the ground.

"Where should we go now?" Issta asked me.

"I don't know," I said. "What's the most beautiful part of Mars to see?"

"How does a mountain three times the size of Mount Everest sound?" Issta asked with a smile. I knew she was talking about Olympus Mons.

Even with wings it would be too tall for us to fly over, but we would be able to fly around it. I would finally get to see it up close after months of gazing at it from a distance.

While we were whooshing high over the red, dusty ground, I thought about how thankful I was that our new friends had come to help us when we needed help most. I knew that eventually we would establish contact with mission control, and they would send a team to take us back to Earth. That would take a few years, however.

Until that time, we had the vaccine to help us survive on Mars. Ultimately, our crew would be known as the first group of humans to live on the Red Planet. I had a feeling that many more people would follow our lead, but only time would tell how they adapted to their strange yet beautiful new home.